W9-CUD-945

BERYL GERDES

FOR MY SON 1989

RYAN GERDES

with all my love forever, Dad.

Guns
IN COLOR

Logan Thompson

Cathay Books

10
107

CONTENTS

A collection of Colt revolvers (endpapers) includes the percussion Army Model of 1860 (top); an 1862 police pistol converted to .38 rimfire (centre); and a .36 calibre pocket percussion revolver (bottom).

A Flintlock Sea Service pistol of 1805 (title page) was used by Royal Navy personnel.

This page shows a United States Star carbine, 1858 pattern (top); a Leach experimental .577 calibre cavalry carbine of 1854 (centre); and a Princes .577 carbine of 1855 (bottom).

INTRODUCTION

Gunpowder, a mixture of sulphur, charcoal and saltpetre, was known to the Chinese by AD 1,000 and was probably introduced to Europe by the Arabs. A firearm can be defined as a tube, or barrel, through which a projectile is propelled, and directed at a target by an explosive force. The first crude models were loaded by pouring gunpowder and bullet into the barrel, then fired by applying a hot wire to the touchhole which ignited the charge.

The matchlock mechanism was invented in the late 15th century. Lock is the word used to describe the firearm mechanism which fires a weapon by igniting the primary and main charges (so called because firearm mechanisms were originally made by locksmiths). Early matchlock patterns were crude. The lock consisted of an S-shaped piece of metal (the serpentine), one end of which held the match, the other forming the trigger. To fire, the trigger end was moved by hand causing the match to move on to the priming charge.

The matchlock enabled firearms to be discharged more easily without the services of a second soldier helping to carry out the loading process. It was fitted to the arquebus, the first firearm to resemble a modern rifle, which was fired from the shoulder.

The ingenious and expensive wheellock mechanism, introduced in the 16th century to overcome ignition problems, was soon incorporated in numerous pistols and longarms. Sometimes these had rifled barrels which caused the missile to rotate in flight thereby achieving greater accuracy. The mechanism worked by means of a clockwork-driven, grooved steel which sent a steady stream of sparks into the priming pan when set against an iron pyrite (replaced later by a flint).

Improvements continued with the snaphaunce mechanism (AD 1540) which comprised a flint-clasping arm sited opposite a hinged plate. On firing, a spring forced the flint down against the plate causing sparks to be directed into the priming pan. This system was more reliable than the matchlock but simpler and cheaper than the wheellock. However, the snaphaunce was in turn soon replaced by the more efficient flintlock in which the frizzen

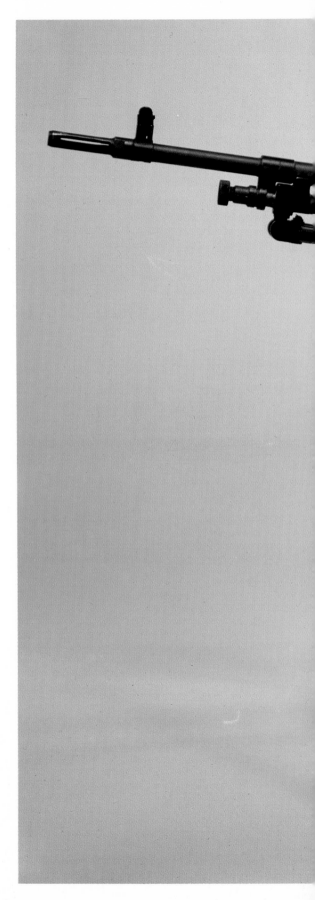

The L7A1 GPMG (general purpose machine-gun) was modified from a Belgium FN design. It fires the 7.62 mm Nato cartridge.

A
200 RDS
7·62 MM BALL L2 A2
LINKS MKI
RG.14.6.67.B

combined the functions of steel and pancover. This had a flint-holding arm (cock) and a steel plate (frizzen) which, when struck by the flint, swung back to expose the pan, creating a shower of sparks which fell into the priming.

Flintlocks had two disadvantages: misfires, and the delay between firing and the bullet actually leaving the barrel. In the early 19th century, a percussion ignition method was invented consisting of a small fulminate-filled cap placed on a hollow nipple connected to the bore (the hole in the barrel down which the projectile travels). This was exploded by the hammer on firing.

During the 19th century, firearms with rifled barrels and percussion ignition systems became the standard military weapon. The introduction of the breech-loading rifle firing a cartridge simplified the loading process, while improved charging compounds increased the range. Rifles which loaded at the breech afforded the soldier greater protection as he could load his rifle while lying down. Various bullet firing systems were invented. The Prussian Dreyse needle gun was the first effective breech-loading weapon. It incorporated a long needle which pierced the fulminate pellet set between the powder charge and the bullet. Rifled barrels, pinfire cartridges, new explosive compounds, and bolt actions enabled rapid loading and unloading, whilst greatly improving firing rate, range, and accuracy.

Automatic weapons developed to increase firing rate and volume. Revolvers, containing an ammunition supply in a revolving drum, successfully increased the firing rate but were not truly automatic. An automatic weapon is one which continues to fire until the trigger pressure is released: whilst a self-loading firearm only automatically reloads after each shot. Machine-guns, producing continuous automatic fire, had first been attempted with the Puckle gun (1718).

Light, semi-automatic pistol development started in 1893 with the Borchardt which developed into the Luger, followed by Maxim, Browning and Mauser pistols. Later, World War I trench warfare conditions introduced the need for a close quarter weapon capable of producing rapid fire. In World War II, the major armies were equipped with heavy and light machine-guns, submachine-guns and single shot or automatic rifles.

The French musketeer (c. 1590) carries a form of matchlock arquebus (right). The .455 calibre Webley revolver (below) dates from 1904 and has served the British in many wars.

MATCHLOCKS AND WHEELLOCKS

Firearms developed from crude handguns with the introduction of the matchlock and then the wheellock mechanisms. The two ball-butted pistols here are inlaid with staghorn. The top pistol (1593) was made in Nuremberg and has a French-type lock with a separate mainspring. The bottom weapon dates from 1579.

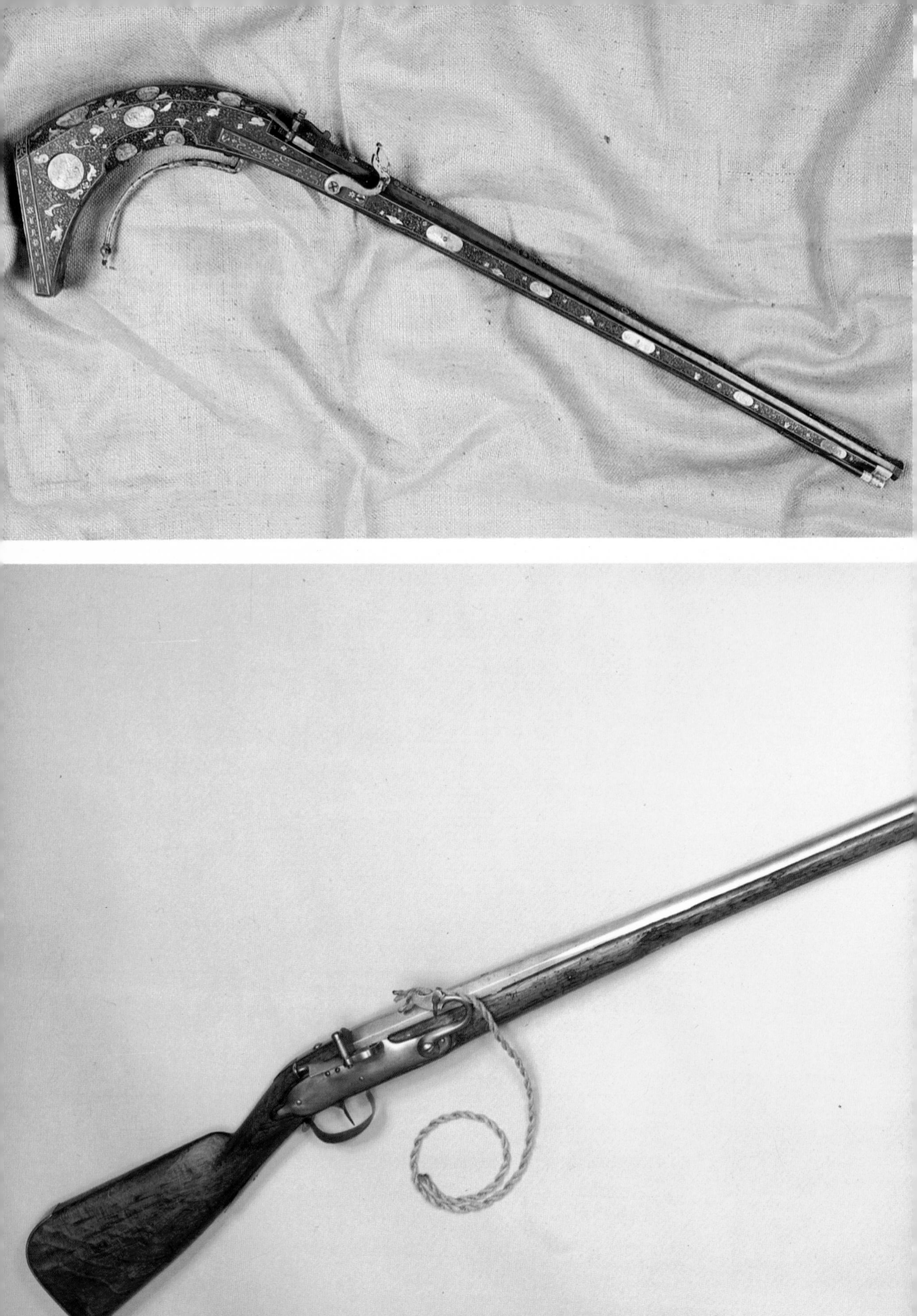

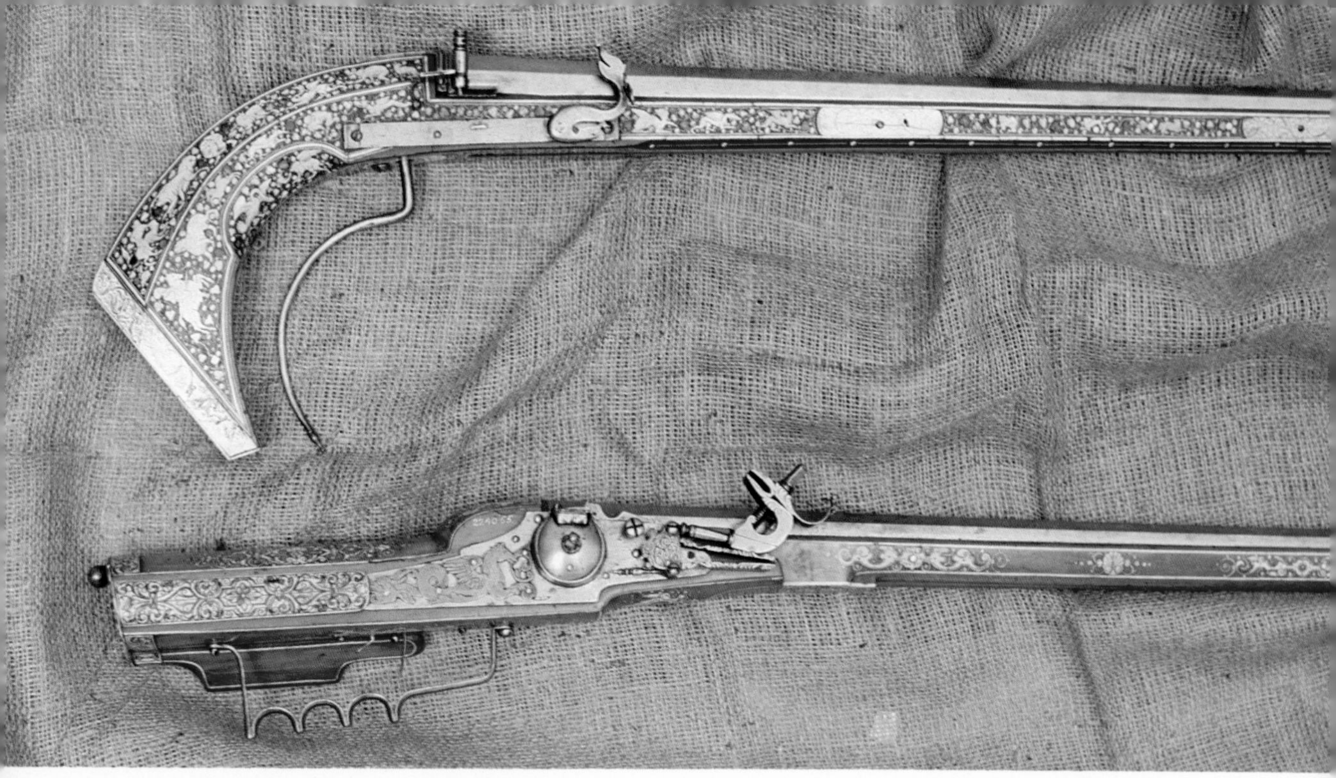

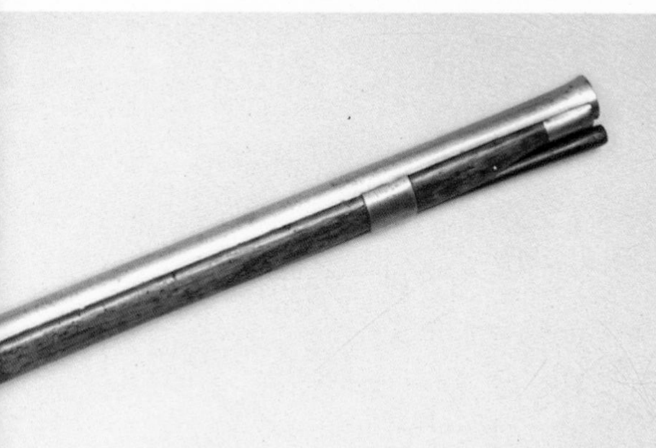

A petronel was a light firearm designed to be held against the chest on firing, hence the sharply curved butt. The continental example (*above left*) is an early one. It dates from the 16th century and is matchlock operated with a long, curved trigger operated by hand. Many of these early firearms were beautifully decorated in contrast to their crude mechanisms and poor performance.

The 16th-century French matchlock petronel (*above right, top of picture*) was obviously produced for a wealthy patron. The ornate and high-quality firearm below it (1605) incorporated the reliable wheellock mechanism which worked on the principle of a clockwork notched steel wheel creating sparks when set against a piece of iron pyrite or flint. The wheel was fitted with a spindle connected by a short length of chain to a powerful mainspring. The wheel was wound with a special key causing the chain to be wrapped around the spindle under tension from the mainspring. On firing, the spring pulled back on the chain, causing the spindle and the wheel to revolve. A 'dogshead' set close to the wheel dropped the pyrite/flint which made contact with the wheel. The sparks created flew directly into the priming pan, igniting the charge.

The robust matchlock musket (*left*) was made in Denmark and its plain appearance is typical of early firearms produced for the general market. This military weapon, complete with ramrod, closely resembles modern rifles in style. Most of the mechanism is housed safely within the stock. The trigger is protected by a guard. Some early muskets had banded barrels and crude sights.

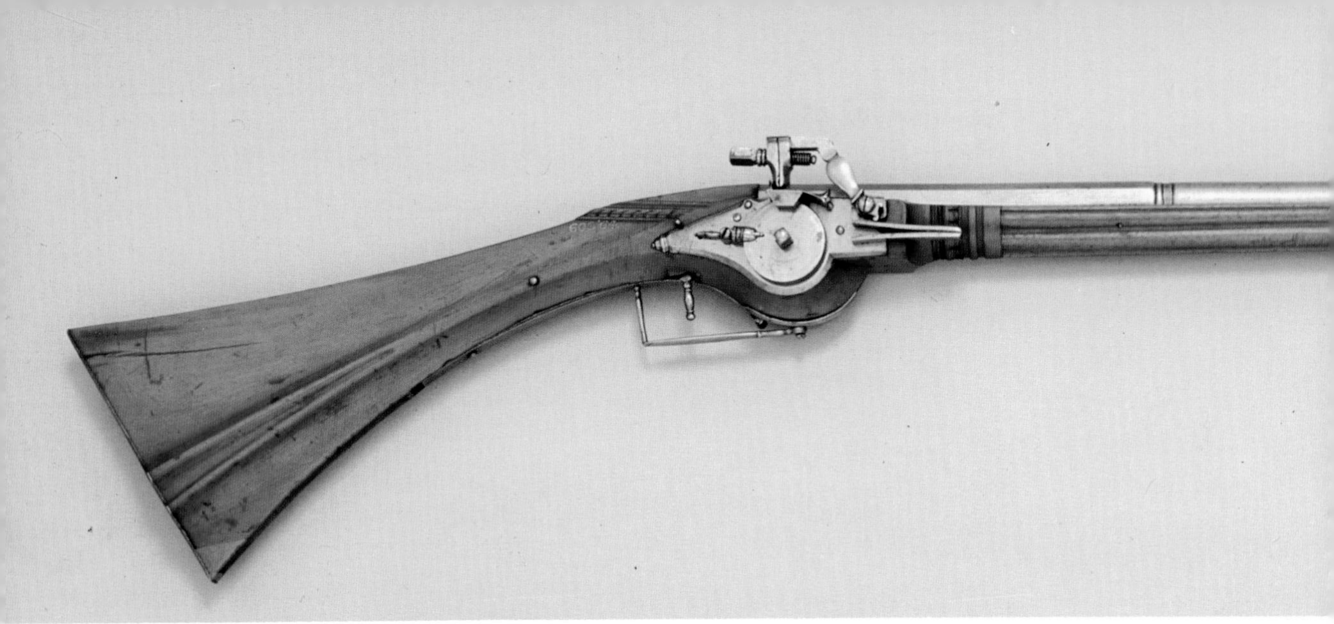

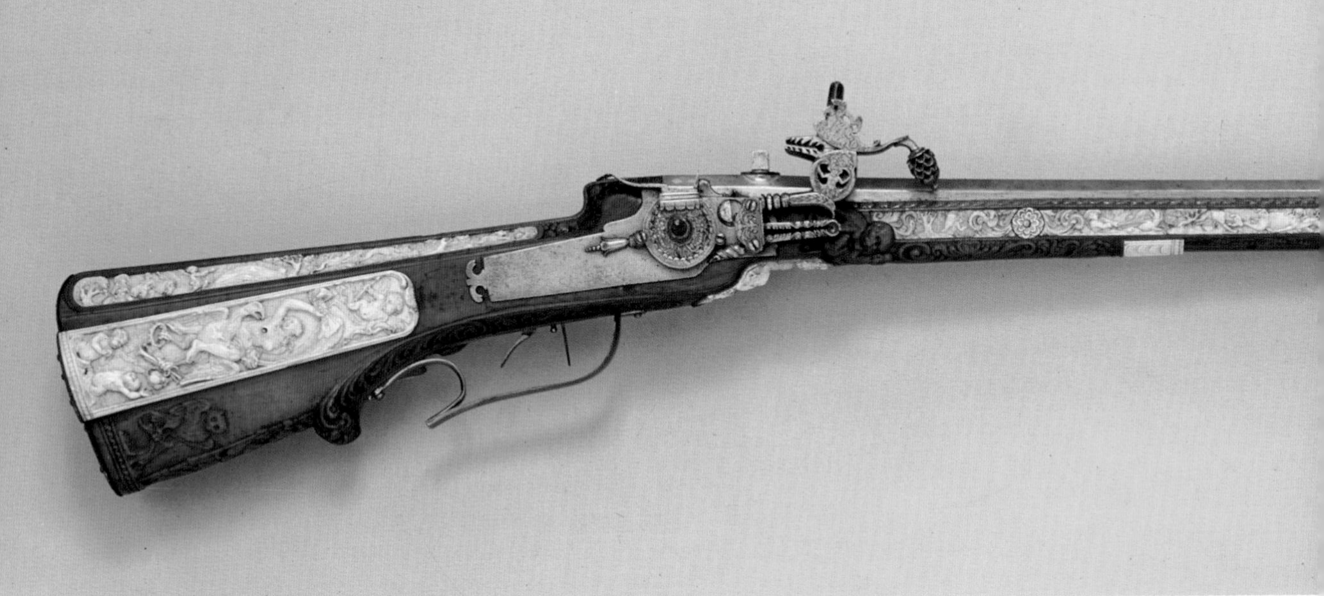

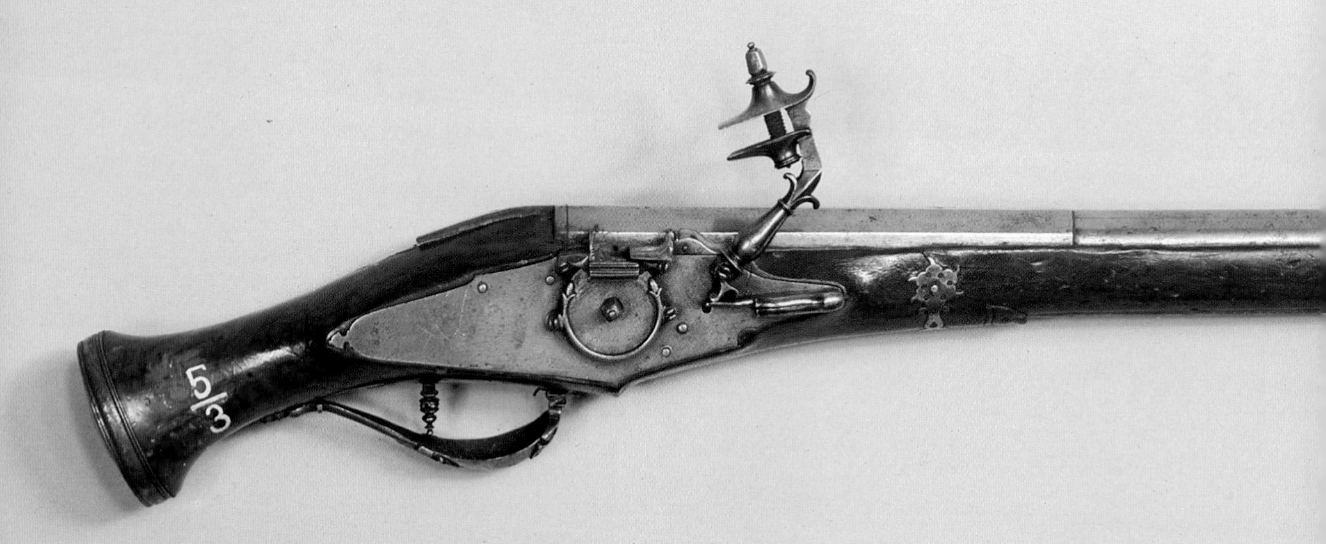
5/3

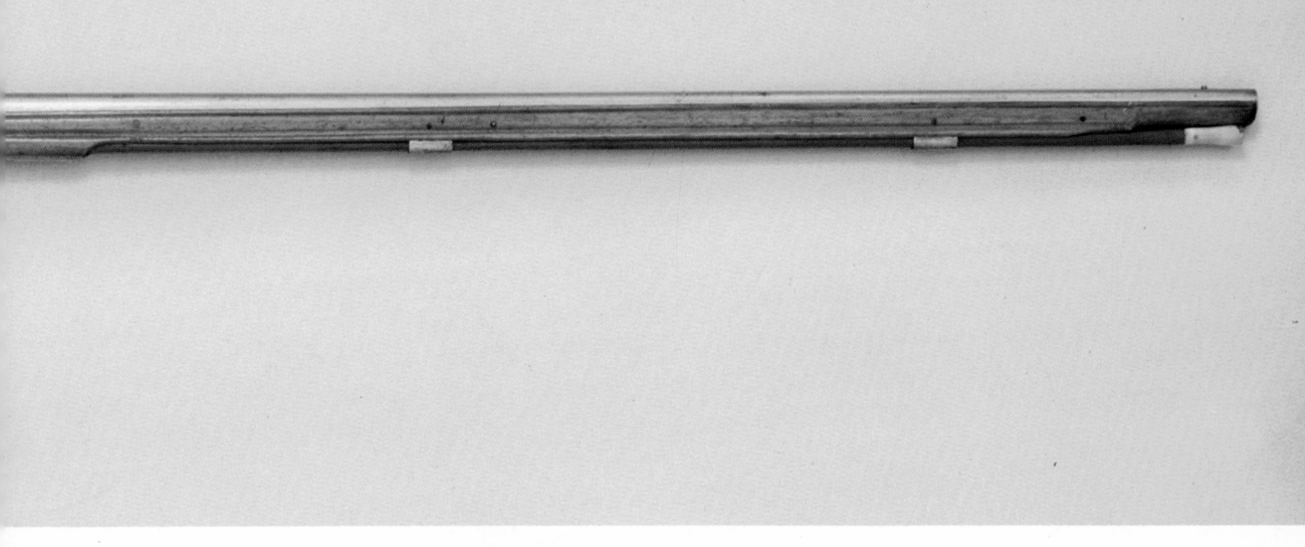

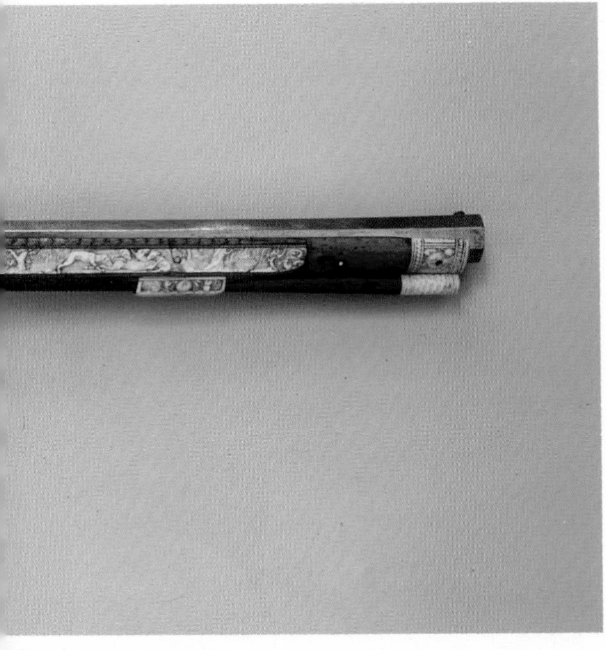

The French wheellock birding piece (1625) (*above*) was made for a youth, probably Louis XIII of France (1601–43). The stock is plain pearwood with iron mounts. Wheellocks were popular with sportsmen and hunters because of their accuracy, and they could be held ready loaded, then sighted and quickly fired before the prey had time to move.

The carved pearwood stock of this south German wheellock rifle (1670–80) (*middle left*) is set with carved ivory panels and signed by the gunsmith, Johann Michael Maucher of Swassich-Gmund. Decorations on this type of lavish and expensive item were frequently enhanced by engraving. Despite the reliability and attractiveness of the wheellocks, however, they were subject to stoppages often caused by fragments of broken pyrite penetrating and obstructing some part of the internal mechanism. The loss of the winding key, particularly in battle, caused an obvious problem. The cost of repair also meant that the matchlock, despite its drawbacks, remained popular as the owner could carry out most repairs himself.

The wheellock pistol (*bottom left*), with its chiselled steel mounts, originated in northern Italy (1625–50). These weapons were the first satisfactory firearms for horsemen because they enabled the rider to control his mount while aiming at an opponent. Firearms which could be retained loaded, however, needed safety catches and these were incorporated in later wheellocks.

RIVIERE

FLINTLOCKS AND PERCUSSION

During the 17th century the flintlock became the standard ignition system and was incorporated in all types of pistol and longarm. The percussion ignition system was a further important development. The two 19th-century flintlock pistols (above) have swivel ramrods. Apart from minor changes the flintlock system was to remain in use for 250 years.

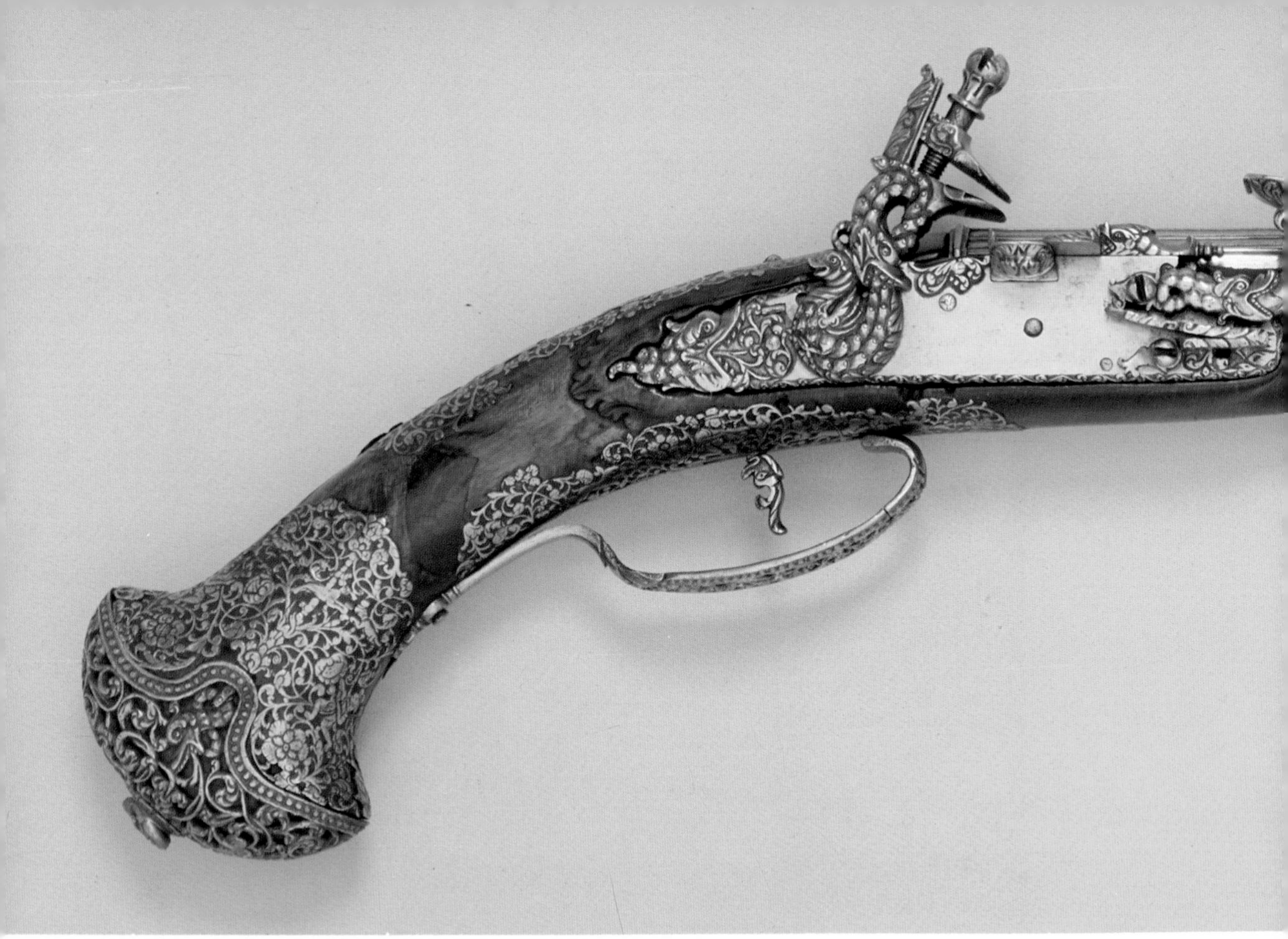

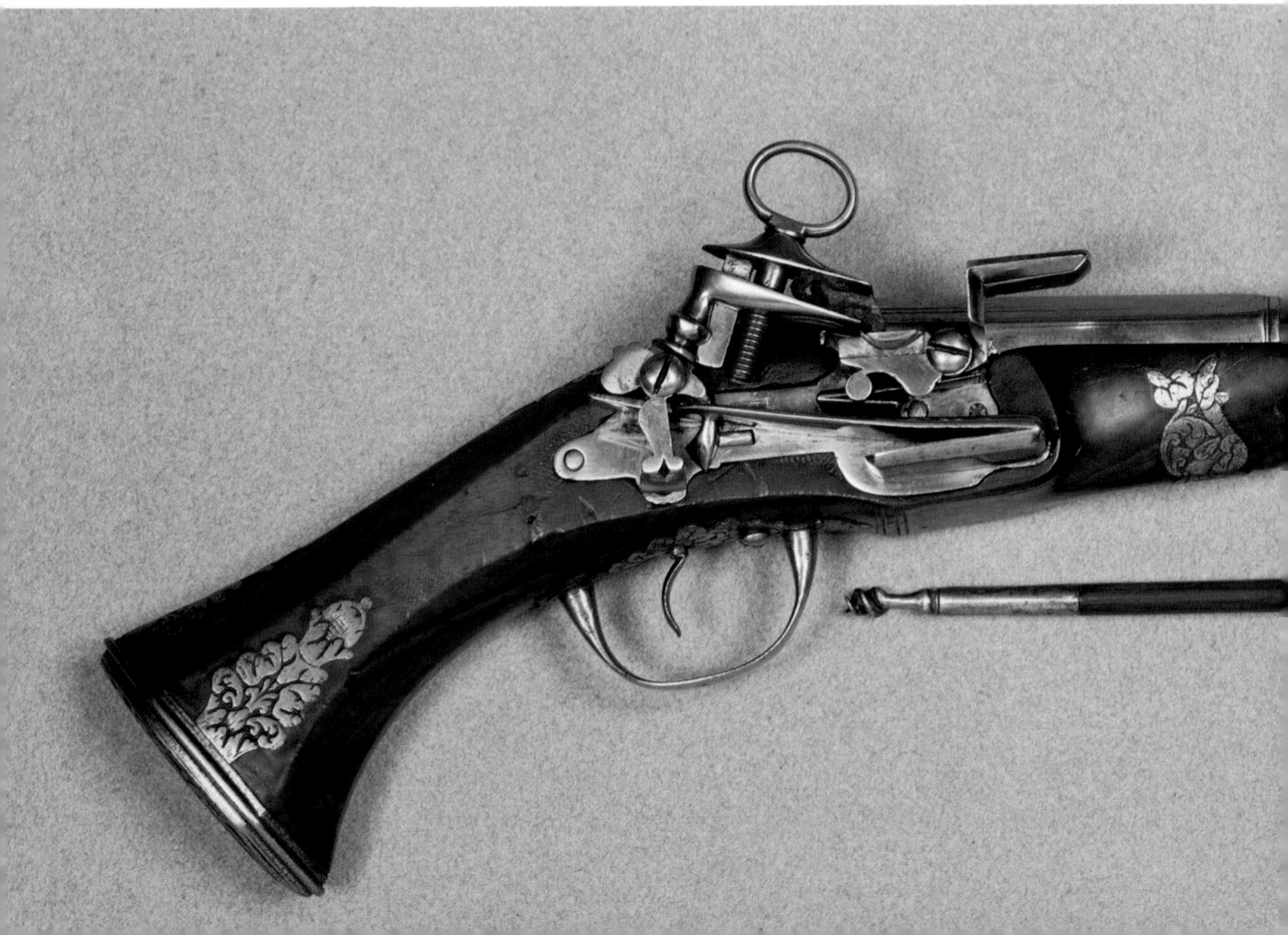

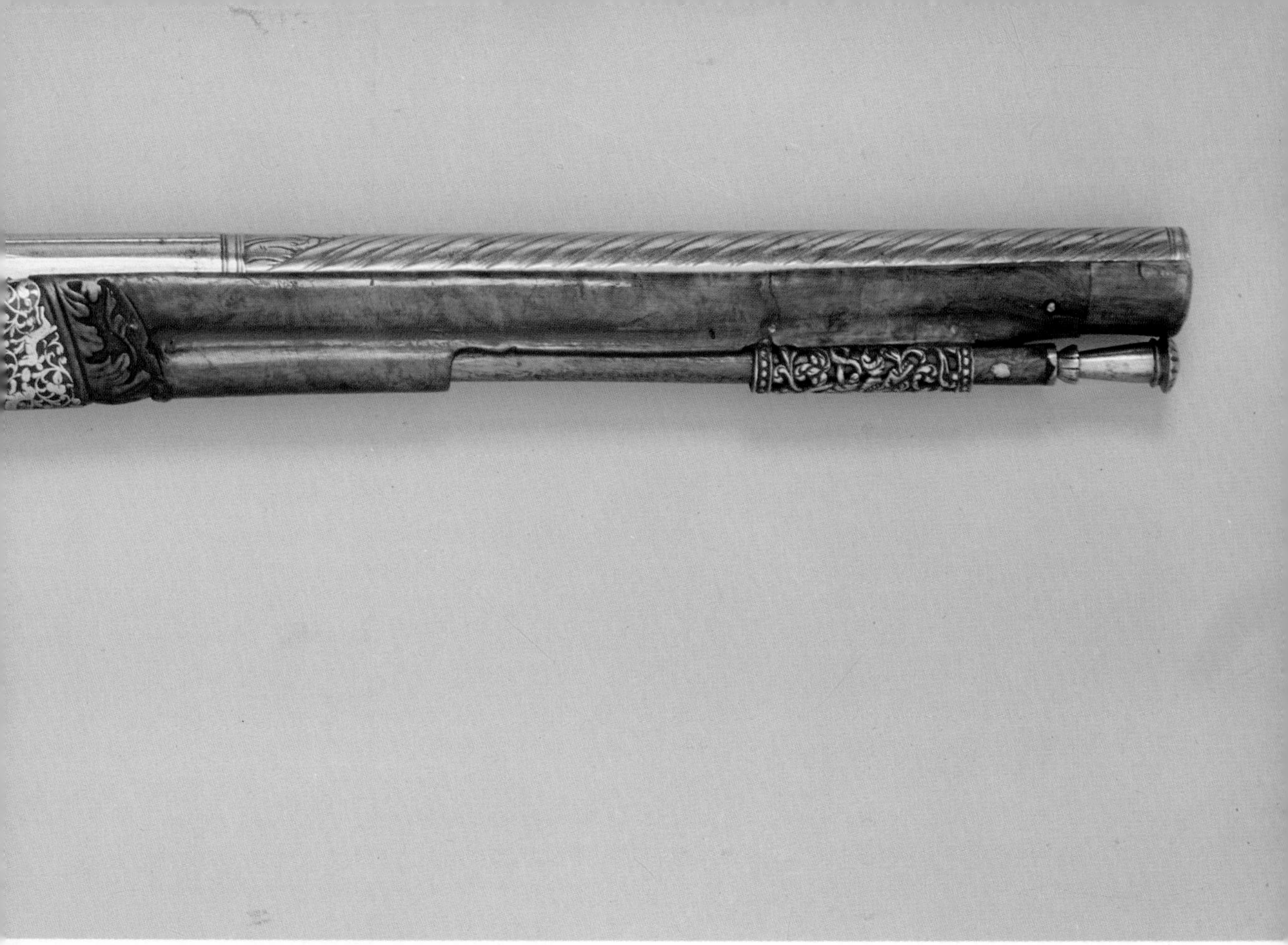

The highly decorated Italian holster pistol (1650) (*above*) was designed to be carried by mounted travellers. The mechanism is snaphaunce with the mainspring housed within the stock and the pan set between the cock and steel. Such mechanisms had more working parts than the later miquelet and flintlock systems. Also, it was necessary to open the pan cover to prime before firing, a time-consuming loading procedure.

The miquelet system (*left*) combined the steel and pan cover into one part, as in the flintlock. It also had a safety device which allowed the cock to be held halfway towards the steel in the 'half-cock' position. The large screw on top of the cock, which kept the flint in position, could be turned by hand which meant that the owner need not carry any other tools. The extremely powerful mainspring was fixed to the outside of the lock plate instead of being housed internally as in the snaphaunce and the flintlock. The ramrod of this particular pistol has a bullet extractor at one end (left hand in this picture). The miquelet with its combined steel and pan cover was really a transitional weapon between the snaphaunce with its internal spring and the flintlock which used both these features successfully. The system developed in southern Europe and was popular in Spain and Italy.

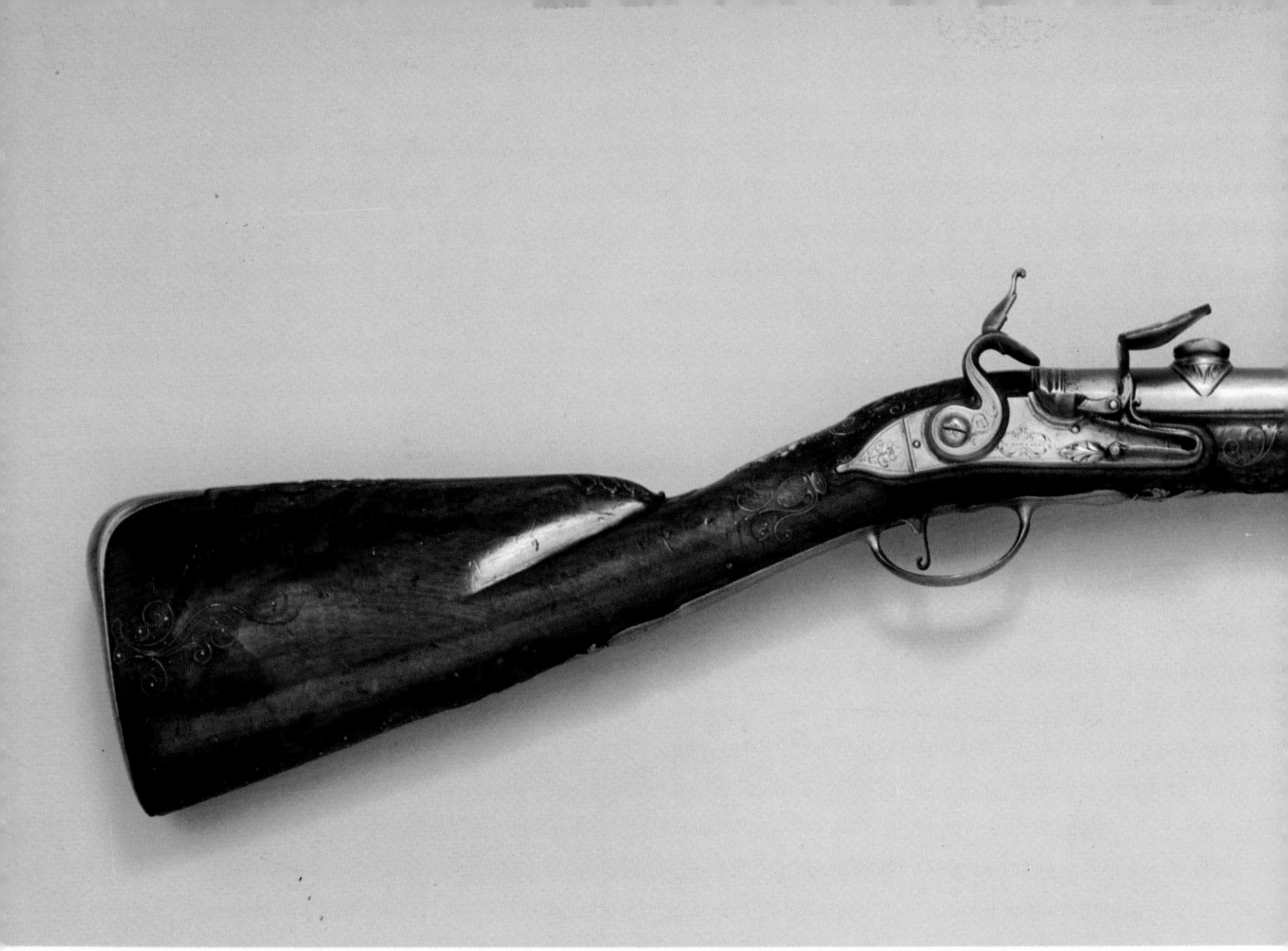

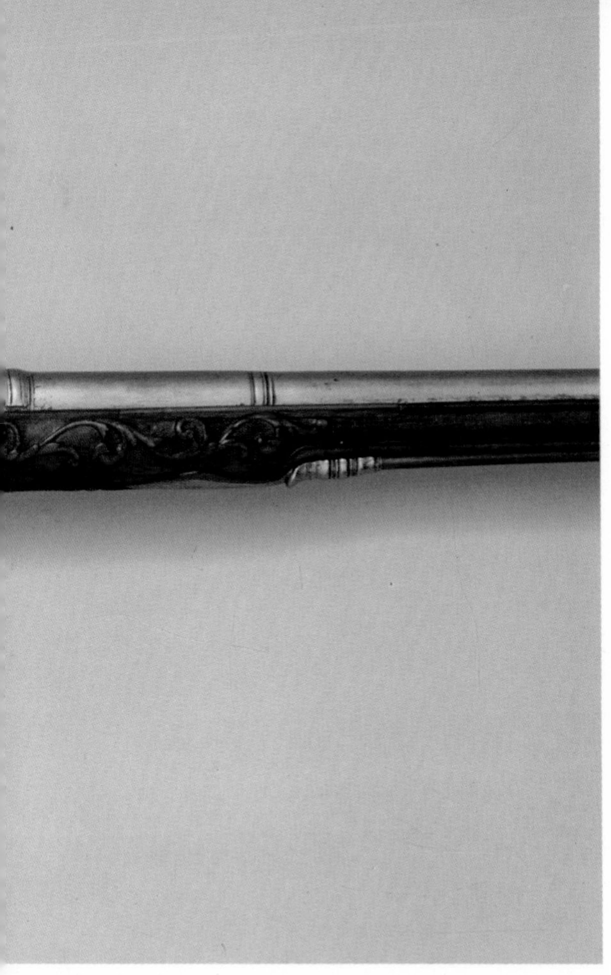

The French loading flintlock-operated sporting gun (*top left*) dates from 1720. The mounts are silver and iron. This gun shows the way in which sporting guns were decorated. The main problem with the flintlock sporting gun was its performance in bad weather. The powder could become damp or blow away, and the time taken for the weapon to actually fire meant that the huntsman had to maintain the correct aiming position for some time. It was also very frustrating if the prey moved away between the time the trigger was squeezed and the missile finally left the barrel. The gun illustrated here has an imported lock mechanism and is signed by R. Rowland, London (1720).

The Russian flintlock fowling piece (*bottom left*) has steel mounts encrusted with gold. The lock is signed by A. Leontiew. This weapon was made in Tula and was probably acquired by an English peer on a visit to Russia. The wealthy frequently regarded their firearms as status symbols and therefore spent vast sums of money acquiring more efficient and attractive weapons. This investment greatly assisted improvements in sighting devices, the development of special barrels and more reliable ignition systems. This technical progress was eventually incorporated in the cheaper weapons for the masses.

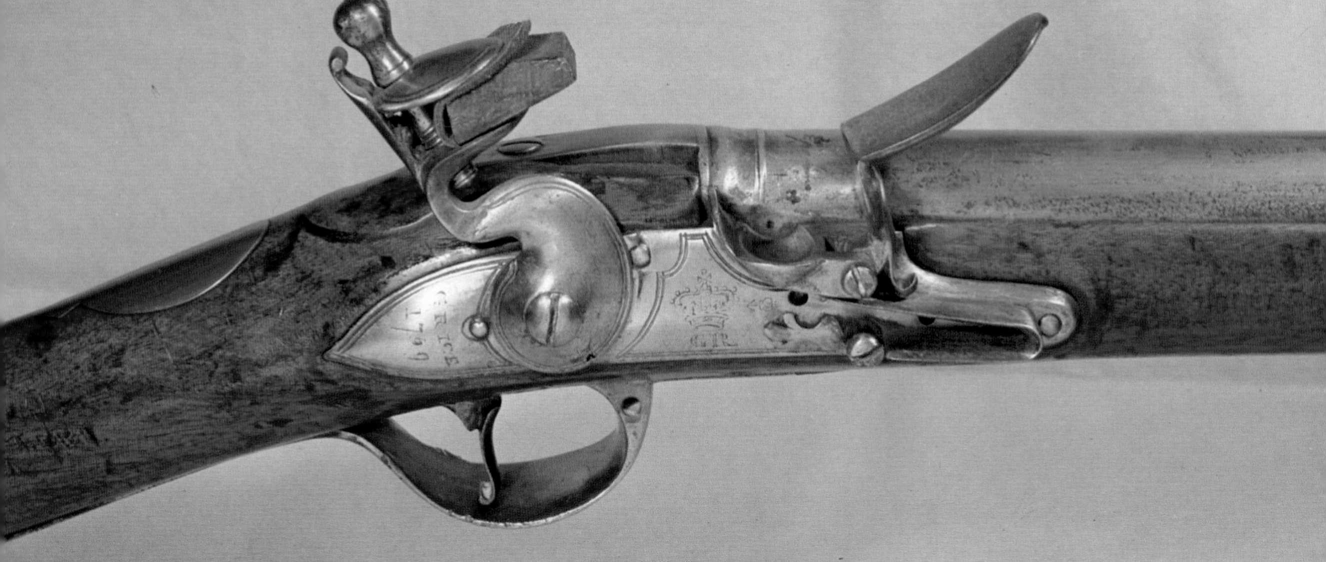

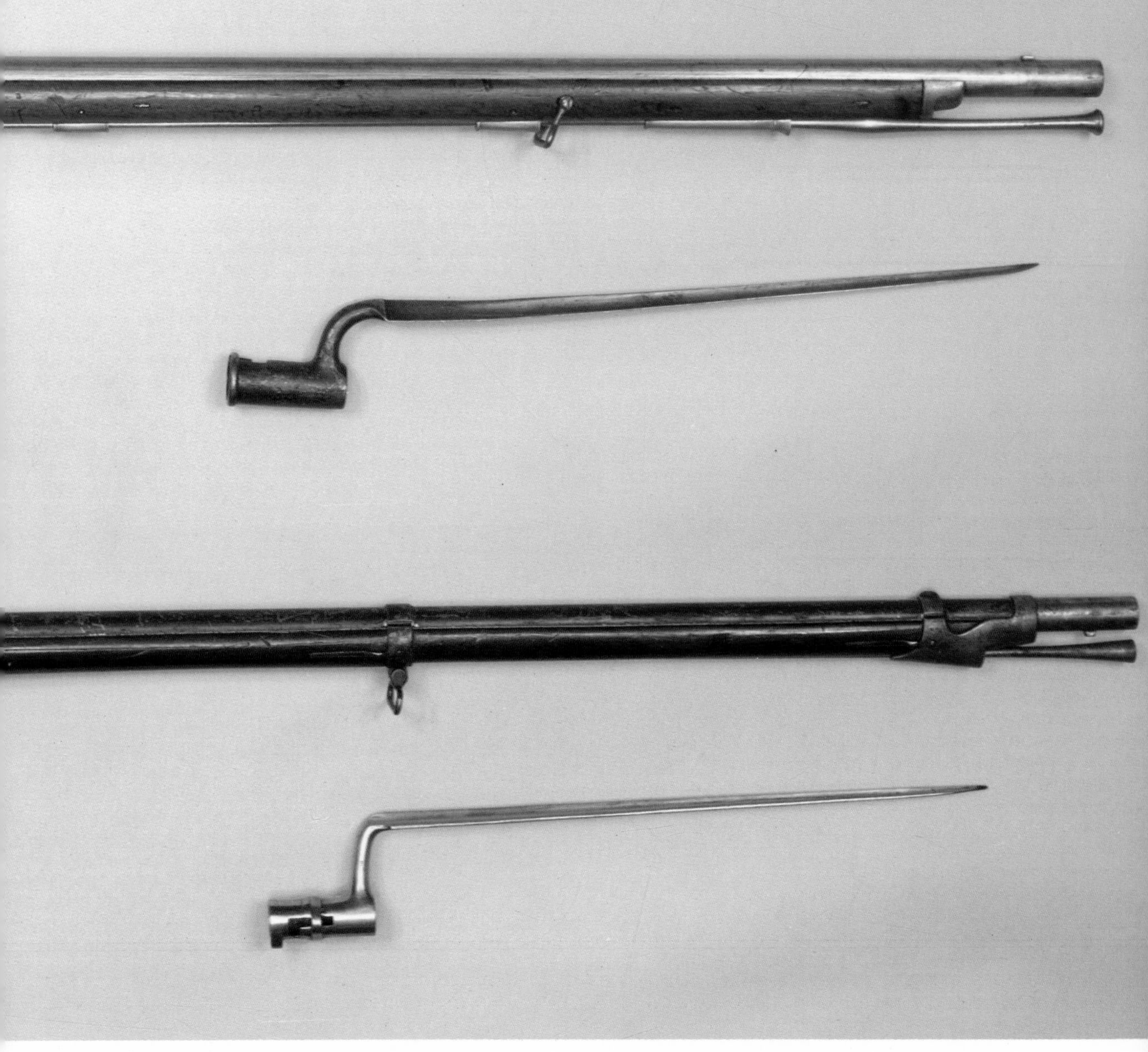

The Brown Bess was the musket of the British army from about 1730–1835. It appeared in eight different patterns. The New Land pattern (1802) is pictured here (*above, top*). The musket was equipped with a steel socket bayonet, which could be kept fixed during firing, and a wooden ramrod was later replaced by a steel one. Early Brown Bess patterns had the lines and balance of English sporting guns. The New Land pattern had a 106 cm (42 in) barrel and a .750 in bore. The British soldiers who used the weapon carried up to 160 cartridges in a leather pouch and two brass cleaning rods for unclogging the touch hole. The cartridges consisted of sealed tubes of strong paper each containing a powder charge and lead ball. To load, the soldier bit the end off a cartridge with his teeth and primed the pan with a small quantity, then closed the pan cover. The remaining powder was poured down the barrel and compressed with the ramrod. Finally the cartridge paper and ball were rammed down on top of the powder. The bullet was smaller than the bore to make loading faster. This was vital as although the Brown Bess was accurate up to 137 m (150 yd), volleys were discharged by ranks at close range on the calls of a drill crier.

The operation and performance of French muskets (*above, centre*) was similar to that of the Brown Bess except that they had the barrel and stock banded together with steel or brass loops.

Lock plates were often marked with the Royal cypher, the word 'Tower', the maker's name and date. The lock on the Brown Bess (*left*) illustrates this practice.

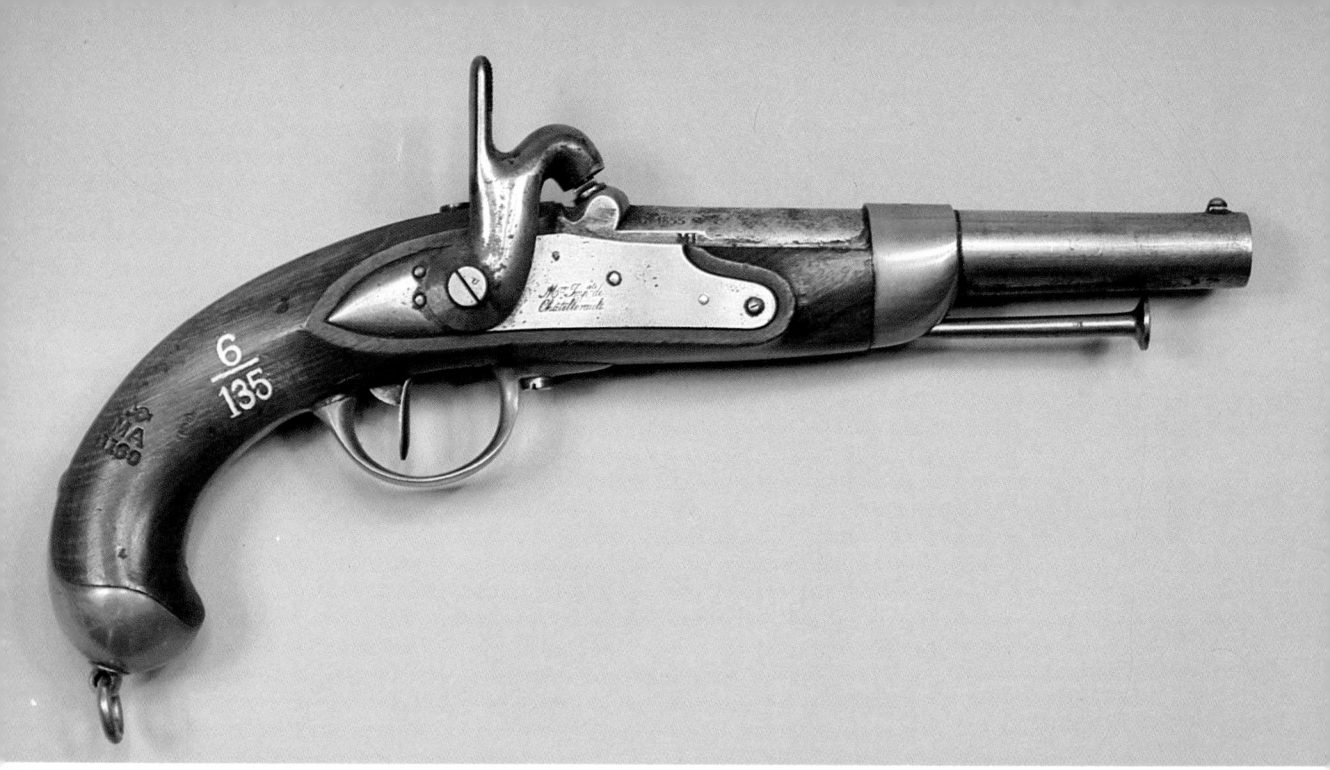

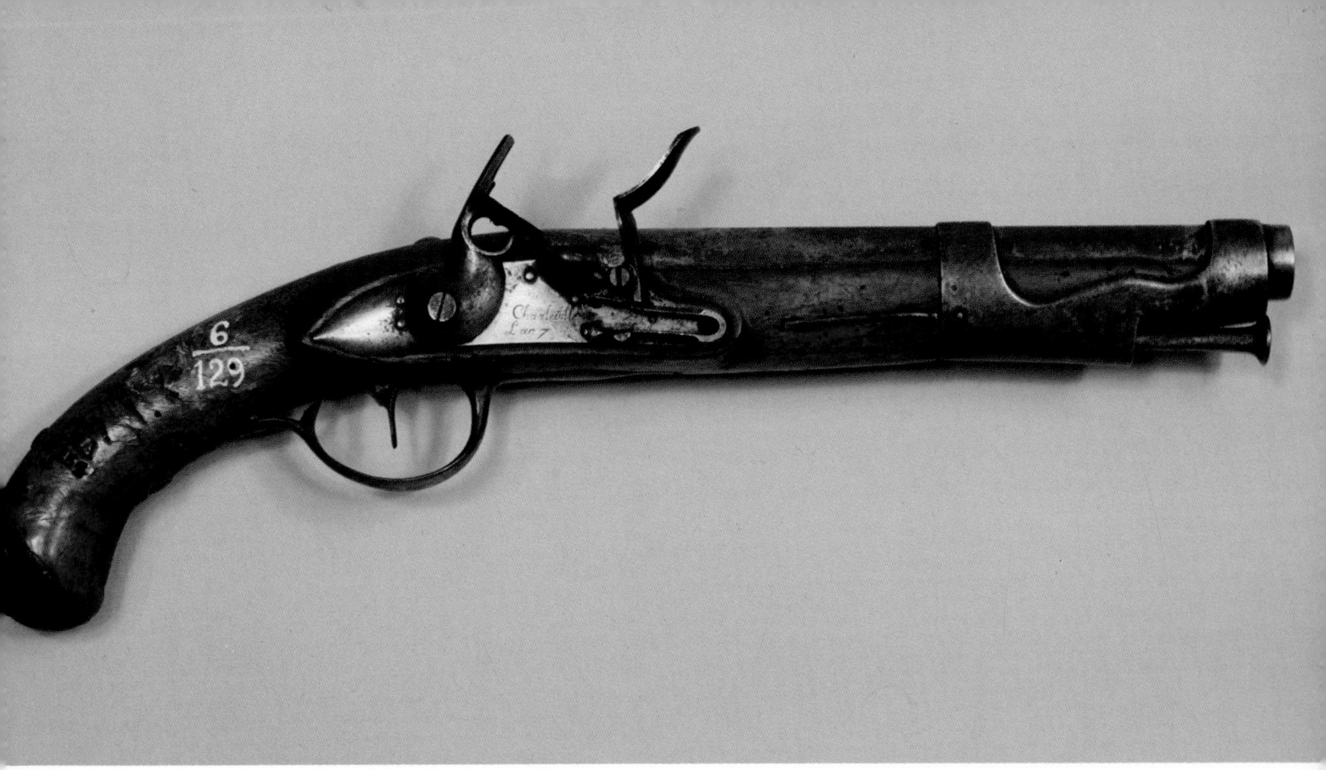

The French percussion cavalry pistol (*top left*) is an example of the way many flintlocks were converted to the percussion ignition system. This particularly applied to military weapons because governments were reluctant to introduce new, expensive weapons while they still had large stocks of flintlocks. Many pistols and longarms were therefore converted to percussion between 1830 and 1860. Cavalry were equipped with these pistols and carbines but they tended to rely on shock tactics and their heavy cavalry sword or sabre for success. The pistols were, however, used at close quarters.

The French military pistol (*above right*) is from the Royal armoury at Charleville, a famous production centre noted for the production of this 1763 weapon. These .70 calibre pistols were carried by the French cavalry during the Napoleonic wars. Cavalrymen had another problem when firing from the saddle. The sword had to be sheathed or kept on the wrist by a sword knot – a further distraction when taking aim.

The French flintlock duelling pistol (*left*) has a rifled barrel inlaid with gold and butt-caps of ebony, and some of the iron mounts are engraved with landscape scenes. The lock and barrel are signed 'Boutet à Versailles' and the high quality of this weapon is typical of duelling pistols. Accuracy up to at least 23 m (25 yd), good balance and reliability were essential in weapons used in close personal combat. Although duelling was discouraged by the authorities, the custom persisted until the early part of the 19th century.

The percussion pistol (1815) (*above*) is fitted with the Forsyth lock with its 'scent bottle' shaped primer. J. Forsyth was determined to reduce the time lapse between squeezing the trigger and the missile leaving the muzzle. He therefore replaced the old flash pan with a steel plug through the centre of which was a tiny hole leading to the interior of the breech and the main charge. Attached to the plug was the bottle-shaped primer divided into two sections, one section containing sufficient primer for 20 shots. When the container was turned halfway round, a small amount of priming agent fell into the pan. It was then returned to its original position, bringing the striker into line with the flash pan.

The compact French gendarmerie percussion pistol M1842 (*below*) has a 12 cm (5 in) barrel and a calibre of .603 in.

The painting by F. Remington (*right*) shows an Indian trapper carrying a flintlock plains rifle. Plains rifle is the collective term given to numerous rifle patterns produced in Ohio, Illinois and St Louis from about 1815 onwards. The settlers who travelled west found that their Kentucky long rifles were not powerful enough to kill the bears, bison and buffalo that they encountered as a heavy bullet was needed to stop these large, fast-moving animals. The plains rifles were the answer. They were generally between 68 and 100 cm (27–39 in) in length, with a .45 to .55 in bore.

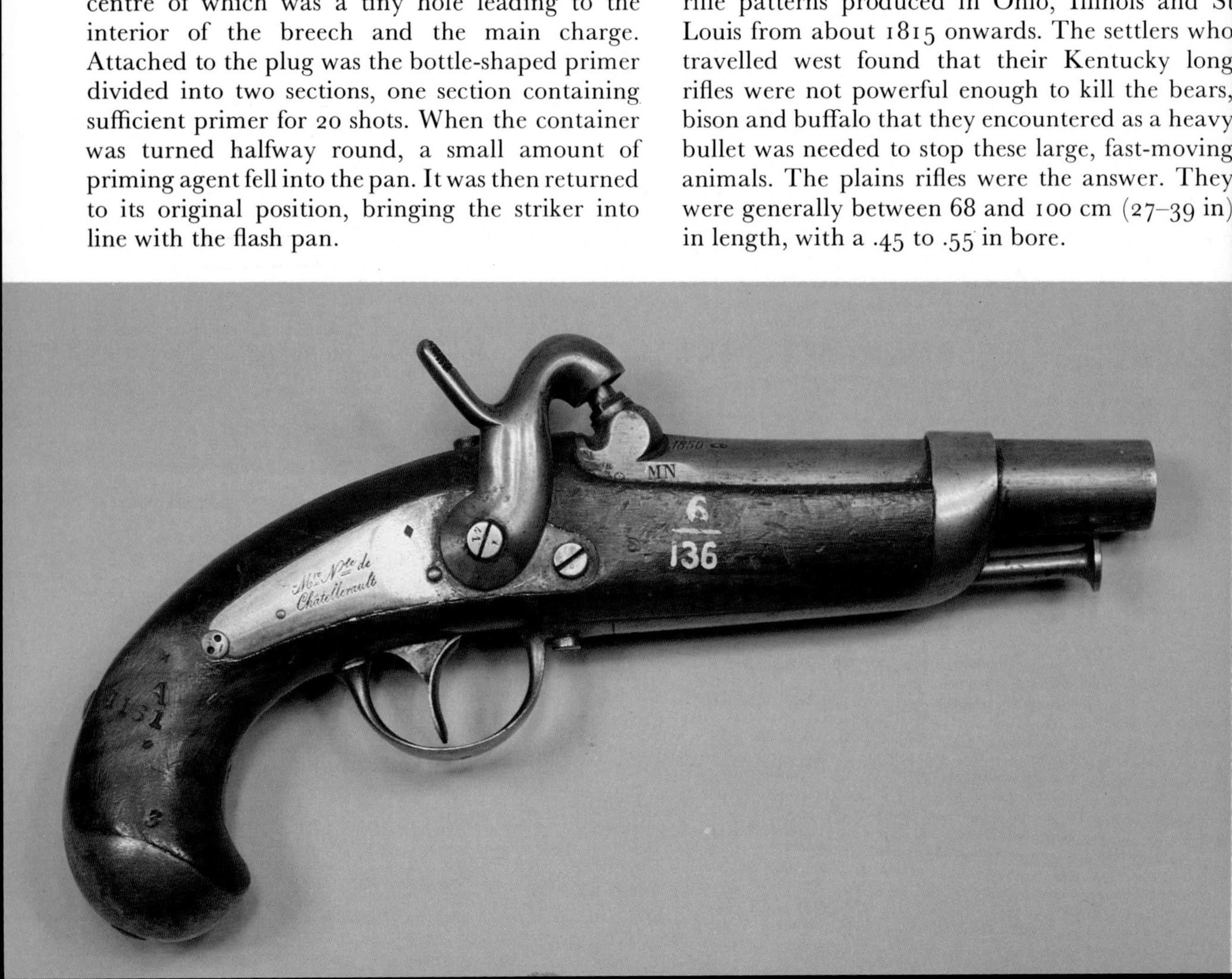

FREDERIC REMINGTON

RIFLES

By the mid-19th century rifles had become the standard military weapon and later breech-loading, bolt-action mechanisms made them a powerful and deadly long-range weapon. The Short Magazine Lee Enfield .303 rifle No 1 Mk III (top) was introduced in 1902 and was probably the best bolt-action rifle ever produced. The Lee Enfield .303 in No 5 Mk I (bottom) was produced late in World War II for jungle fighting in the Far East.

ENFIELD

The Dreyse needle rifle (*top left*) was designed by J. N. von Dreyse in 1827. It was the first successful military breech-loader, and was adopted by the Prussian Army in 1840. The cartridge, containing bullet, ignition substance and powder, was placed in the breech and secured by closing the bolt. A long, spring-actioned needle pierced the cartridge and this activated the fulminate cap which was set between the main charge and the bullet. The explosion ignited the charge forcing the bullet out of the barrel. Problems arose if the needle broke and sometimes gases escaped from the imperfectly sealed breech. Prussia used the rifle successfully in wars against Denmark (1864), Austria (1866) and France (1870–1). This success forced other nations to adopt similar rifles as the bolt action made reloading in a concealed prone position much easier.

The British Snider rifle (1861) (*left, top*) was a .577 in bore rifle converted from the Enfield rifled musket of 1853 illustrated in a further converted form (*left, bottom*). Both weapons are almost identical. The breech system designed by Jacob Snider was based on the Dreyse gun but it had better breech sealing and less likelihood of needle fracture. The 1853 percussion rifle was used by the British army during the Crimean war and the Indian mutiny. The cartridges used by this weapon contributed to the mutiny as rumours spread among the Indians that they were greased with the fat of cows and pigs.

The French Chassepôt rifle (1866) (*above*) was a much improved Dreyse-type rifle fitted with a long, curved, brass-hilted sword bayonet. The weapon was automatically cocked when the bolt was closed and the firing pin was stronger.

The Winchester lever action rifle (*above*) was produced by the Winchester Repeating Arms Company which specialized in repeating rifles. The standard model had been designed by B. Tyler Henry and was known as the Henry rifle. Although the name had changed the first model in 1866 was very much a Henry but the modifications enabled it to be fired at a rate of 30 rounds per minute. This was followed by the 73 and then the 76 patterns. The 1873 model was a centrefire which used the 44–40 cartridge.

The rifles were famous for their extremely fast reloading process. This involved a tube magazine containing 15 cartridges and a lever action connected to the trigger guard which cocked the hammer, pushed cartridges into the breech and later ejected the empty case. The magazine spring forced the top cartridge against the movable block, and when the trigger guard lever was pulled down (as here in the picture above) a cartridge was taken from the magazine and the hammer cocked. Raising the lever forced the cartridge into the breech. The rifle could fire one .44 rimfire smokeless powder cartridge in 2½ seconds.

The French colonial trooper (*right*) is seen with his Lebel rifle (1886) (*overleaf, top*). The weapon was named after Lieutenant Colonel Nicholas Lebel, a member of the commission which selected the new weapon for the French army. It was the first small bore (8 mm) rifle using a cartridge with a smokeless propellant. It had a tube magazine containing eight rounds and an efficient bolt action – when opened a cartridge raiser brought up a new round, lining it up with the chamber. On closing, the bolt pushed the cartridge home and cocked the fixing pin. In 1890 the tube magazine was replaced by a box type. The rifle, with its slender hexagonal-shaped, pointed bayonet, was used by the French army and the French Foreign Legion in north Africa.

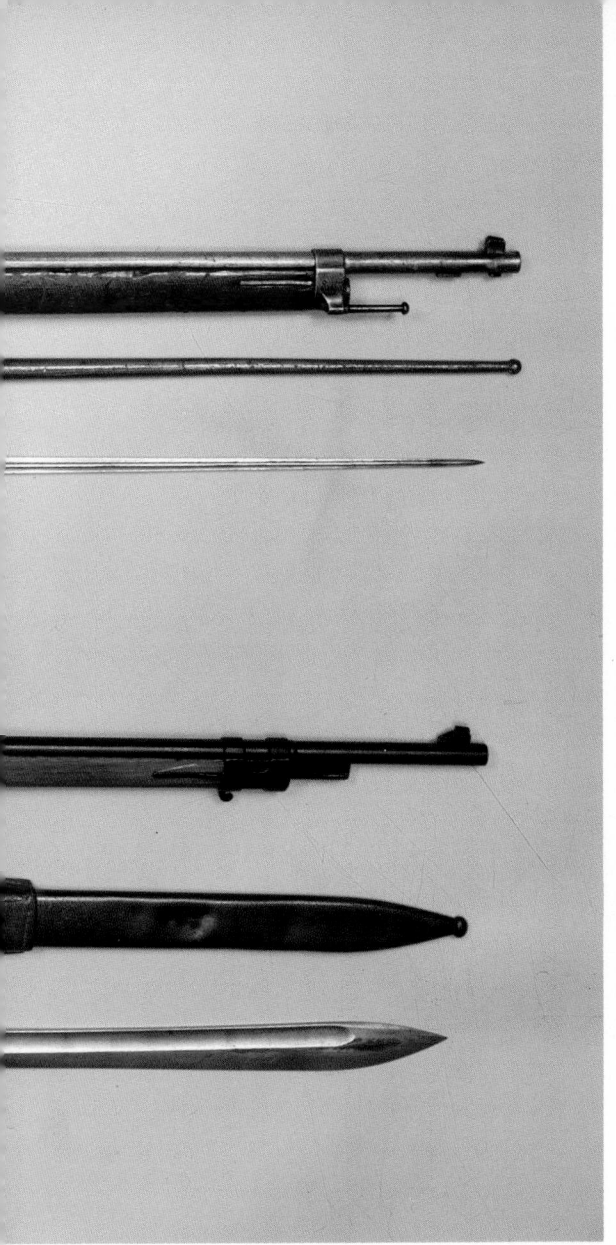

The French Lebel rifle (1886) (*left, top*) replaced the 11 mm Gras rifle (1874). The Mauser German infantry rifle M1898 (*left, bottom*) is the famous German rifle which was in service with the German army in various amended forms until 1945. The Mauser brothers adopted the von Dreyse bolt action and improved it before including it in their infantry rifle of 1871 which they produced in large numbers and which established their reputation. The next Mauser (M1884) had an even better bolt and an eight cartridge tube magazine fitted under the barrel. Later well known patterns included the Turkish M1893 and the Boer rifle M1895. The accuracy and long range of the Mauser rifles was essential because armies now fought at much greater distances from each other and they were usually supported by powerful long range artillery. The British learned this lesson during the Boer war when they were fired upon by a hidden enemy using Mauser rifles. They suffered enormous casualties and so they changed their uniform colour to a drab khaki and trained their men to fire accurately from a distance. The results of this training produced a small, regular, trained army which prevented defeat in the first year of World War I. The 1898 rifle (pictured here) was equipped with a heavy single-edged sword bayonet complete with metal scabbard.

The US Garand rifle No 1 .300 in (*below*) was designed by J. C. Garand who worked for the Springfield armoury in Massachusetts. The rifle was developed by 1931 and taken into military service in 1936. The self-loading, gas-operated rifle went into mass production in 1939 and was used extensively by American forces during World War II. It weighed 4.2 kg ($9\frac{1}{2}$ lb).

REVOLVERS

A revolver is a firearm with a cylinder comprising a series of barrels or chambers – each loaded – which revolve, and can be turned to align with the hammer. This enables several shots to be fired quickly without reloading. The Colt .455 New Service revolver (above) was produced in great quantities between 1898 and 1944. Its balance and frame made it very accurate.

The two flintlock revolvers (*below*) are by Elisha Collier, an American gunsmith from Massachusetts who produced the first practical pistol with a revolving chamber in 1818. The cylinder was turned by hand to align the barrel with the flintlock cock. There was a very clever priming mechanism in which the single priming pan was recharged after each shot by a magazine fitted on to the priming pan cover. When the pan closed, it operated a ratchet and pawl device. The pistols were smooth bore and muzzle loading.

The early pattern (1819) had the manually operated cylinder of five chambers and was the first revolver to have the ratchet-operated primer and internal cock (top gun). The second pattern (1820) had an external cock and a fluted cylinder.

The Collier revolvers, though good, were expensive and the American industry could not support their production. Collier therefore went to England.

The English pepperbox pistol (.38 in bore) by Parkhouse of Taunton (*right*) was typical of many such pistols produced in the early 19th century. Pepperbox pistols developed as a means of increasing the firing rate and providing an available ammunition supply. The pepperbox was first introduced at the end of the 18th century with a flintlock mechanism, and on early models the barrels were turned by hand to align the chamber with the bar hammer. On percussion models, each barrel had its own nipple upon which was set a cap which was exploded by the hammer. On most patterns the squeezing of the trigger caused the barrels to rotate. These pistols were satisfactory at close quarters but because of the weight of the barrels in relation to the short overall length, they were very unbalanced. There was also a tendency for the ignition of one cap to ignite the others. The pistol was usually sold in a wooden case.

The five-shot, double-action, solid-frame revolver *left*) was made in 1856 by William Tranter. It has a bore of .44 in and has been richly decorated in Delhi. The revolver was muzzle loading and a ever for this purpose, showed open in the picture, vas retained when not in use alongside the barrel. n 1853 Tranter had patented a revolver with two riggers; one for cocking the revolver, the other for iring the weapon.

The transitional revolver (1850) (*right*) had a ix-chambered pepperbox frame and a single barrel. This improved accuracy.

Robert Adams was a British producer of high-quality firearms. They were strongly made, barrel and frame being fashioned from one piece of metal. n 1855, an idea of Captain F. B. E. Beaumont was ncorporated in an Adams revolver (*below*) which enabled the weapon to be either single or double action. Double action is when the hammer is cocked and fired by one pull of the trigger. This is nore useful in battle as the weapon is quicker and easier to fire at targets.

In 1848 Colt produced a .31 calibre Baby Dragoon (*overleaf*) which proved so popular that in 1849 it was modified and remained in production vith slight changes until 1873. This weapon dates from 1849, and is London made.

pieces, lay down the parts
what you took out last.
near the Hammer
it downwards out of the
Trigger, the Sere Spring
returning each of the

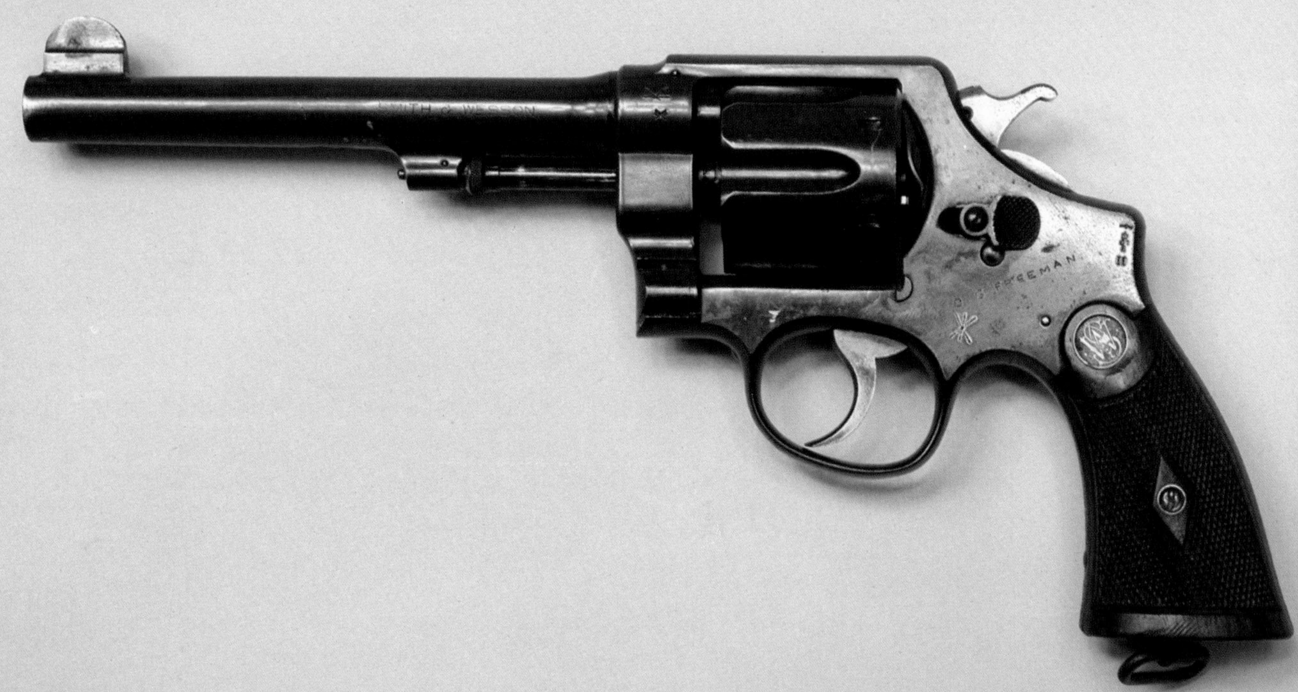

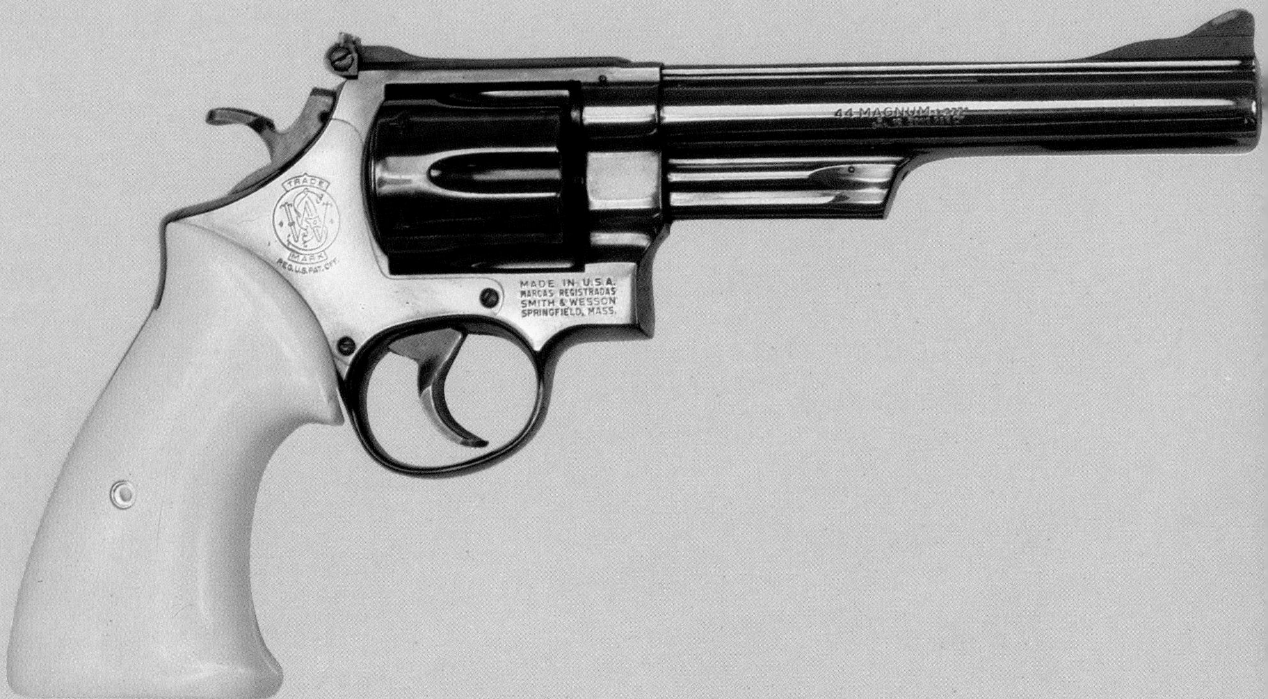

44 MAGNUM
MADE IN U.S.A.
MARCAS REGISTRADAS
SMITH & WESSON
SPRINGFIELD, MASS.

The Smith and Wesson Gold Seal model (1907) *above left*) was a .455 calibre revolver with six hambers operated on the hinged frame loading nd automatic ejection system which worked by he action of the barrel being swung down. It was roduced by the Smith and Wesson Company, an merican firm set up in 1854. The double-action, wing-out cylinder of the Smith and Wesson design s now the standard revolver type.

The one area in which the revolver has undisputed uperiority over the self-loading pistol is that of ower as it can use much larger cartridges. The evelopment of the so-called magnum cartridge, irst in .357 calibre, then in .44, has produced the losest thing to a hand cannon. Although the recoil s difficult to manage, the .44 Magnum (*left*), here roduced by Smith and Wesson, is the most owerful production handgun in the world.

The Enfield revolver No 2 was produced in two patterns. The Mk 1 .38 calibre (*above*) has both single and double action, while the Mk II is double action only. Both patterns were used by British forces until the mid 1960s when they were superseded by the 9 mm Browning self-loading pistol. The Mk I has a built-in safety device that makes the hammer rebound away from the cartridges after firing. It has a rifled barrel and six chambers set in a revolving cylinder. The weapon is of the hinged frame type which means that both barrel and cylinder hinge forward for reloading. When it was discovered under scientific and combat conditions that the .38 in bullet could stop an advancing target as effectively as a .455 calibre weapon, the Enfield replaced the British Webley .455 in as the standard service revolver in World War II. Even after being dropped in water it operated effectively.

FAMOUS GUNS

There are many well-known weapons whose names are easily to pick out when talking of famous guns, and the six featured here are instantly recognized.

THE KENTUCKY RIFLE

This rifle was first made by German immigrants to the United States who had settled in the Pennsylvania area. Manufacture on a large scale started about 1720. Early patterns were probably copies of the Jaeger rifle so successfully employed in Europe, particularly by the German rifle corps. Originally, the weapon was a powerful one intended for hunting wolves, bears and boars in thickly wooded country. Weighing about 4.5 kg (10 lb), it was muzzle loading, flintlock operated and fired a heavy bullet. Soon the rifle changed to suit local requirements in the eastern American region. Settlers wanted a weapon for shooting deer, not big game. Furthermore, they preferred a lighter bullet to reduce carriage weight and economize on lead – at the time a difficult commodity to obtain. Therefore, during the period 1740–60 American gunsmiths reduced bore size, whilst increasing the powder charge to improve range and achieve a flatter and more accurate bullet trajectory. The weapon consequently changed: barrels lengthened to 102 cm (40 in), and then to 122 cm (48 in), with smaller bore (the hole in the barrel down which the projectile travels). A patch box was sited in the butt to hold greased linen patches in which the bullet was wrapped before it was rammed into the barrel. This procedure reduced compression loss on firing. This excellent rifle was ideal for small game hunting and defence against Red Indians.

COLT .45 SINGLE-ACTION ARMY MODEL REVOLVER 1873

This firearm was invented by Samuel Colt, an American, born in Hartford, Connecticut in 1814. A solid frame design was introduced as the open frame of the early Colts was too weak for the more powerful cartridges. This made possible the use of .45 calibre ammunition. Soon the model was produced in various calibres and barrel lengths from 7.6 to 40 cm (3 to 16 in). The .45 was the most famous revolver ever produced by Colt, and has continued in production, almost without a break, until the present day. The 1873 weapon is charged with six cartridges in a revolving cylinder operated on a single-action system in which the hammer has to be drawn back with the thumb in order to cock the weapon. Squeezing the trigger causes the hammer to fall forward and fire a cartridge. Such weapons have a slower firing rate than double-action patterns where trigger pressure simultaneously cocks the weapon and turns the cylinder, and immediately thereafter allows the hammer to fall.

This sturdy, accurate weapon with its effective stopping power and ability to continue operating even after being dropped in mud or sand, became very popular. The American army took 37,000 into service, many of which were used in the major Indian campaigns. It was also widely used by outlaws and sheriffs including Billy the Kid, Hickok and Wyatt Earp.

MAUSER RIFLE – M1898

This rifle was produced by the German Mauser company which was developed by the brothers Paul and Wilhelm Mauser. The rifle was the most efficient of a succession of Mauser models spanning a period of 40 years. In modified forms it remained in service with the German army until 1945. As a most successful military weapon it was also widely employed throughout the world and is still the action on which the finest sporting rifles are built today.

The rifle weighed 4 kg (9 lb), and used a 7.92 mm rimless, brass cartridge with lead core bullet which was enclosed in a steel envelope covered with cupro nickel. The magazine was a vertical box type, charger loaded, holding five cartridges in two rows. A length of barrel at the muzzle end was exposed, that is, it was not protected by woodwork. The rifle used the

:ock-on opening bolt system for the first time.
The M1898 was of excellent quality and :xtremely accurate at very long ranges. It erved the German army well in both world vars, and was ideal for use in the prone position - the purpose for which it was designed. Iowever, the rifle was somewhat front-heavy ınd was cumbersome to raise to the shoulder for . standing shot. In 1908, the Mauser carbine 1898 Carbine) was introduced, a shortened orm of the M1898 rifle.

.UGER 9 MM SELF-LOADING PISTOL M1908

\ forerunner of this weapon was designed by Iugo Borchardt, a German emigrant to the Jnited States, and produced in 1893. This ncorporated toggle-type arms, set at the rear of he weapon, which performed the ejection and eloading actions on recoil. Georg Luger leveloped the weapon and his improved version vas produced in 1898. This used a 7.65 mm :artridge, later replaced by 9 mm which ecame standard issue ammunition for ubmachine-guns and pistols.

The Luger is a very high quality weapon, :xtremely accurate up to 68 m (75 yd). The nechanism incorporates a rather large number f components produced to high standards. This roved to be expensive to make under wartime onditions. Overall length is 22 cm ($8\frac{3}{4}$ in), arrel length is 10 cm (4 in), and weight is 50 g (30 oz). Some patterns have differing pecifications, in particular the artillery model vith a 20-cm (8-in) barrel. The magazine apacity is eight rounds. All parts on the .65 mm models, except the barrel, are nterchangeable with 9 mm patterns. The Luger rip is firm and reassuring whilst the wide rigger reduces the possibility of a left or right ull on firing. Excellent sights further contribute o shooting accuracy. The weapon was used uccessfully throughout both world wars, and is till employed militarily by those who prefer a igh quality pistol.

THE THOMPSON SUBMACHINE-GUN

This weapon, better known as 'The Tommy Gun', was designed by the American General J. T. Thompson and first marketed in 1921. This high quality submachine-gun with its forward stock, pistol grip and butt, operated on a delayed blow-back action. The mechanism incorporated the Blish lock, an H-shaped piece which simply provided a form of delayed blow-back. It was replaced on later models by a plain bolt. The air-cooled weapon could fire either single, or automatic shots and was fed by a drum magazine containing 50 rounds. The latter were replaced by a box magazine holding 20–30 rounds. The rate of fire was initially 1000 rounds per minute causing a resupply problem which meant it was not suitable for military purposes.

In 1927 the US Marine Corps accepted the gun (Model 1928) into military service. Its rate of fire had been reduced to 800 rounds per minute. However, it was not until World War II that sales rose. In 1939, the British and French ordered large quantities and the weapon was taken to France by the British Expeditionary Force. It was a popular weapon, ideal for close quarter and street fighting. It is perhaps best remembered, however, for its use during the 1920s in running battles between US revenue men and bootleggers.

RUSSIAN ASSAULT RIFLE – AK47

The 7.62 mm Russian assault rifle was introduced in 1947 and incorporated features developed by the Germans in their automatic rifle, the MP44. This handy rifle, with chrome-lined barrel, is gas operated and capable of single shot or automatic fire. The well-designed weapon was produced in extremely large numbers and used by the Soviet army and those guerrilla groups supported by them. Its specifications are a rate of fire of 800 rounds per minute and a weight of 4.3 kg ($9\frac{1}{2}$ lb). The rifle incorporates the characteristics of both rifle and submachine-gun.

WAFFENFABRIK MAUSER
OBERNDORF A. NECKAR

AUTOMATIC AND SEMI-AUTOMATIC WEAPONS

Rapid fire can be delivered by automatic weapons, which reload and fire continuously as long as the trigger is pressed, and by semi-automatic weapons which fire and reload each time the trigger is pressed. The Mauser military pistol (above) has a 10-round magazine and is sometimes referred to as the 'Broomhandle'.

The Gardner machine-gun (*left*) was invented in 1874 by W. Gardner of Toledo, Ohio. It comprised two breech loading barrels set in line some 3 cm ($1\frac{1}{4}$ in) apart and closed by two sliding breech-blocks. The gun was manned by two men; one fed the ammunition down the slotted feed lane while the other turned the crank. When one breach was closed the other was open, firing the barrels alternately which produced a rate of 300 rounds per minute. The British army and navy took the two- and five-barrelled patterns into service in 1882.

The Gatling gun was invented by an American, R. J. Gatling, who patented a quick firing gun in 1862. The US army officially adopted the gun in 1866. The mechanism (*below*) consisted of six revolving barrels each with a separate bolt, cocking and firing system. Cartridges were fed into a hopper from which they were then inserted into the barrels where a cam caused the moving strikers to fire the cartridge. The entire process was operated mechanically by turning a crank which caused the barrels to revolve. The rate of fire was about 300 rounds per minute. General Custer had the opportunity of equipping his force with Gatling guns before his final campaign in 1876: had he done so, the result at the battle of Little Big Horn might have been very different.

The .45 calibre Thompson submachine-gun (*top*), better known as the 'Tommy gun', gained fame during the 'Roaring Twenties' in America when American gangsters fought the police and each other to protect their illegal dealings in prohibited alcohol. As a close-quarter weapon it was deadly. It could fire up to 700 rounds per minute. The drum magazine, seen here, was eventually replaced by the box type magazine. If not for the war in 1939 these weapons would only have been produced in small numbers, but when the war broke out large numbers of the Thompson were purchased by the British and American armies. It was expensive and rather heavy, but was well made, and proved popular with the infantry and particularly with special forces, such as saboteurs. The Thompson is also produced as a single-shot weapon.

The Sten gun (*bottom*) was produced by the British to overcome the shortage of submachine-guns in the early years of World War II. The weapon was crude and utilitarian and was designed to be produced quickly and cheaply. It was made the official army issue close-quarter weapon in 1940 and although of adequate design, the hasty and cheap construction tended to result in mechanical faults and failures. It was produced in several patterns (the Mk 3 is shown here) and the production of the Mk 2 alone exceeded 2 million units. These were distributed to partisan and resistance groups in German-occupied Europe. The weapon used 9 mm ammunition fed from a 32-round magazine though in practice only 27–28 rounds were loaded to ensure steady breech feed and avoid stoppages.

The Schmeisser MP40 submachine-gun (*centre*) typifies the high quality of the equipment issued to the German army in World War II. The weapon was developed from the MP38 and was first issued in 1940 (hence its name, *Machinen pistole* 40). It was originally intended for use by parachutists, but its efficiency caused it to be widely issued to infantry and tank crews. The operation method was blowback so that when the weapon is cocked the breech-block is pulled right back compressing the return spring. Immediately the firing pin strikes and fires the round. The magazine takes 32 rounds of 9 mm cartridges. The total weight of the weapon with the magazine fitted is about 4.8 kg (10½ lb).

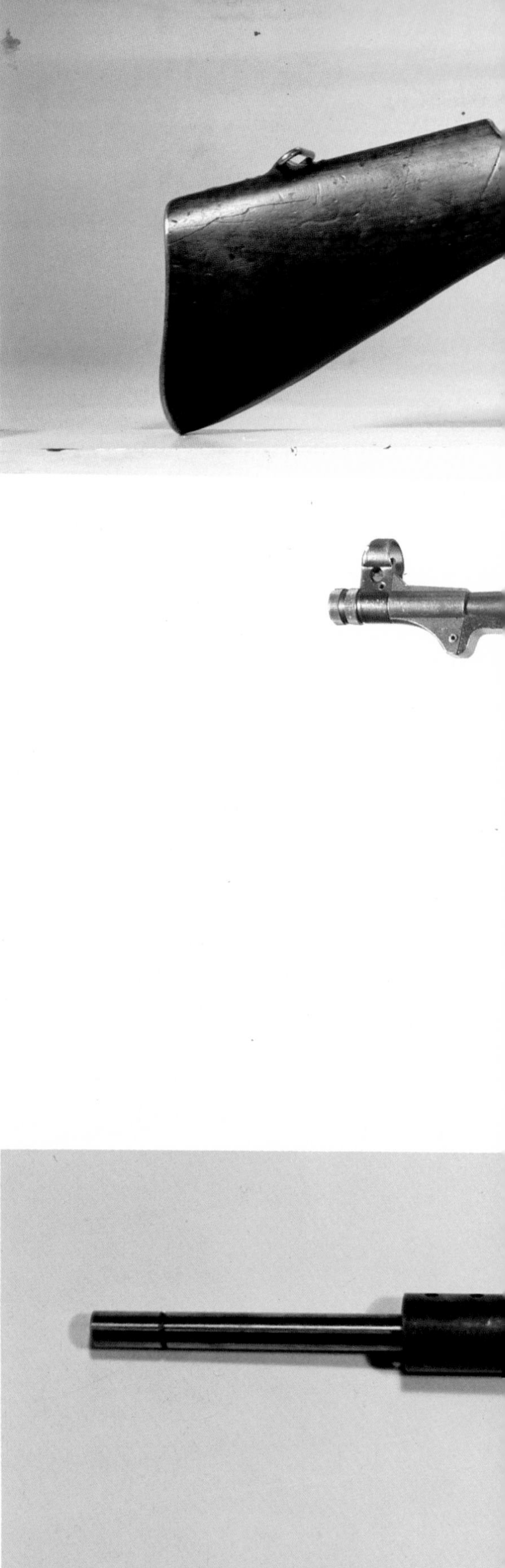

The 7.62 mm Russian pistol (*above left*) was designed by F. V. Tokarev and produced from 1930. This was a modified version of the Browning design and the weapon's mechanism is basically the same though the Russians incorporated improvements which simplified maintenance. The cartridge chosen for the pistol was the 7.62 mm Tokarev, which was a copy of the 7.63 mm Mauser but with a higher propellant charge. Firing, therefore, is often accompanied by flames from the muzzle. It had an eight-round magazine and was used by the Russians during World War II.

The Nambu automatic service pistol Type 94 (*above right*) was the standard issue small arm of the Japanese forces in World War II. It was first produced in 1934 but because of the under-powered cartridge and the poor quality of the components in some of the factories, it was a poor weapon. The 8 mm ammunition was interchangeable with the earlier Model 14.

The Luger Artillery model 08/14 Parabellum (*right*) was an accurate and high-quality recoil-operating weapon with a 19 cm ($7\frac{1}{2}$ in) barrel. It was a version of the Luger Parabellum 1908 model. The weapon can be fitted with a shoulder stock and a snail magazine containing a maximum of 32 rounds. The Artillery version also has a longer barrel – 20 mm (8 in).

火
安
十四年式

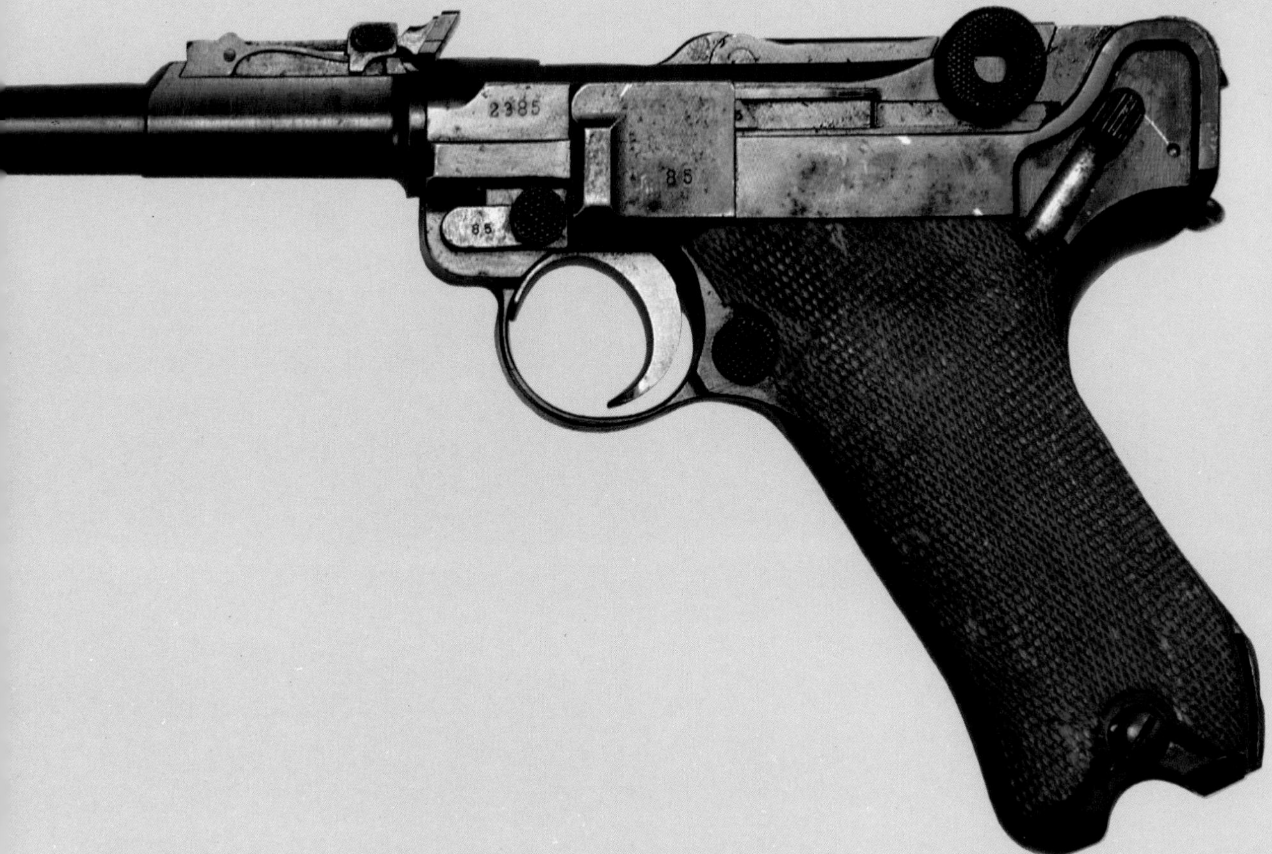

2385
85
85

Beretta is a famous name in the world of guns. The company was established as a family concern as early as 1680 and now employs 16,000 people in an up-to-date production line which makes all parts of the weapons for which they are justly famous. Beretta started making military pistols in World War I and the Beretta Model 34 pistol (*below*) is the successor to their first pistol, the 7.62 mm Model 1915. The most recognizable feature of the Beretta type is the exposed portion of the barrel between the slide nose and the breech. The cartridge for the Beretta M34 is the 9 mm short, and the pistol had a simple blowback action with an exposed hammer. The 7-round box magazine fed a rate of fire of 20 rounds per minute. One disadvantage was that the sights could easily be moved and become misaligned, thus causing inaccuracy.

The Walther P38 (*Pistole* 38) pistol (*top right*) was first issued in 1940 to replace the high-quality and more expensive Luger. It has some unusual design features. The weapon is double action and the hammer need not be fully cocked to be ready for immediate action. This means it can be carried loaded quite safely, with the hammer down. The overall length is 22 cm ($8\frac{1}{2}$ in), it weighs 964 g (34 oz), and the magazine contains 8 rounds. It is semi-automatic and recoil-operated. The Walther was not the only pistol used by the Germans in World War II; the Mauser, Luger and Sauer weapons were all retained in service. German industry had been unable to produce sufficient quantities of the expensive Luger, and this resulted in the mass production of the Walther. Its design was ideal for quick and cheap production. It was one of the first double-action automatic pistols.

John M. Browning was an American gunsmith who could simplify the ideas of others into practical forms. The Browning range of pocket pistols not only started trends in pocket-pistol design over the years but also brought about two designs that are still in use today. These are the Hi Power and the Colt .45 (*bottom right*).

The novel design went through several patterns before the American army accepted the Colt Model 1911. A major change was the adoption of the 1911A1, pictured here, which featured a modified safety grip. The 7-round magazine of .45 in cartridges fed a mechanism which became standard for Colt automatics. The model 1911A1 continued in production throughout the war and reached a total production during that time of over $2\frac{1}{2}$ million.

FN produced this Browning 6.35 mm automatic pistol (*overleaf*) for short-range self defence.

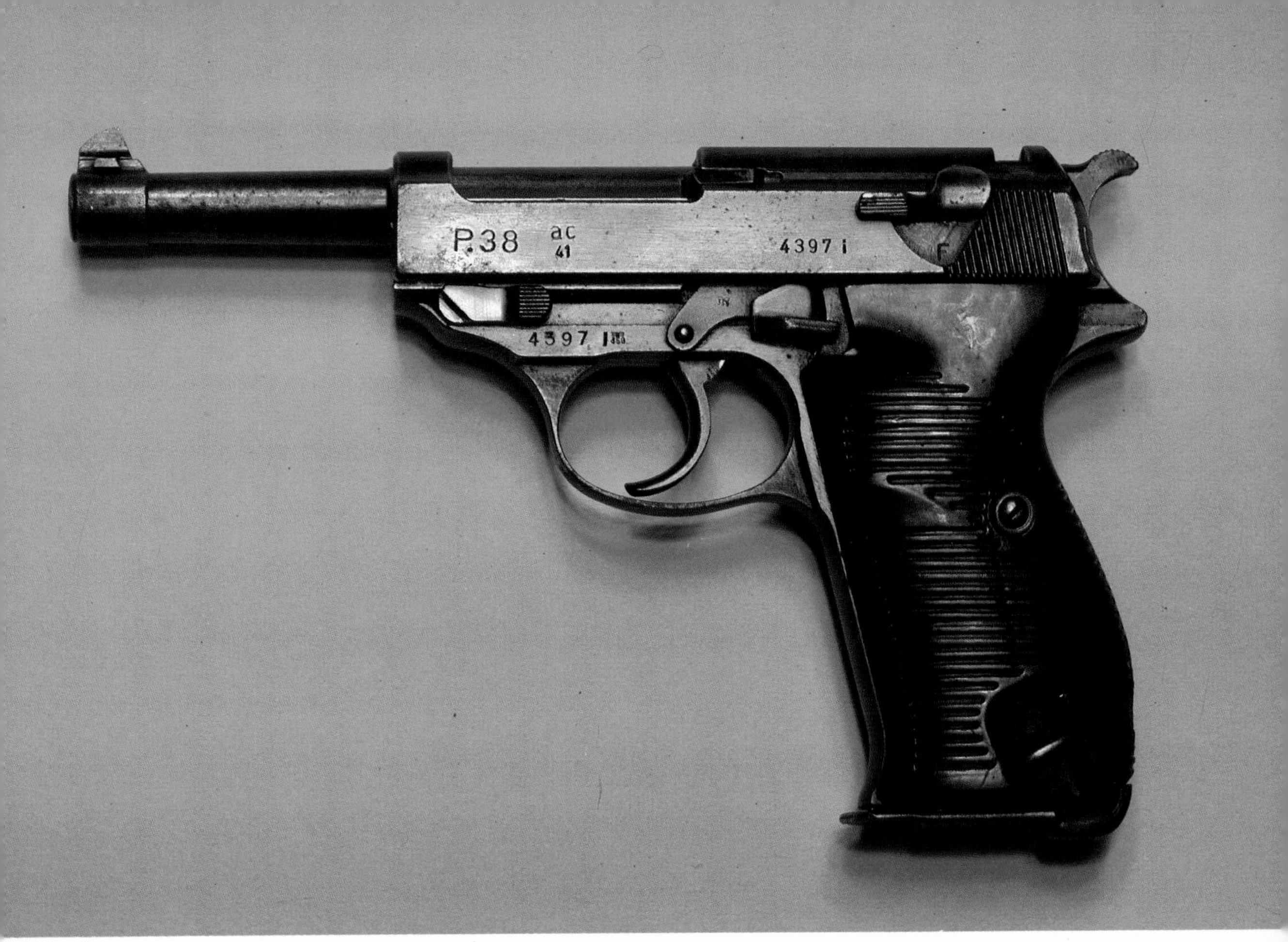

P.38 ac
41
4397 i
4397

PATENTED APR.20.1897. SEPT.9.1902
DEC.19.1905. FEB.14.1911. AUG.19.1913
COLT'S PT. F. A. MFG CO.
HARTFORD. CT. U.S.A.

INDEX

Italicised numbers refer to illustrations

Acknowledgements
Special photography by Angelo Hornak at Holland and Holland Ltd., the Tower of London Armouries and the Museum of Artillery, Woolwich.
The Cooper-Bridgeman Library 8–9, 12–13 above, 12–13 middle, 16–17 below, 18–19 above and below, 22–23 below, 36, 52–53 below; Ehrlich Tweedy Archive Ltd. 20, 50–51 below; Mary Evans Picture Library 7 Gunshot Picture Library Title Page, 10 above, 11 above, 28 above, 28–29, 29 above; Holland and Holland Ltd. (Angelo Hornak) 42 below, 64; Angelo Hornak Endpapers, 30 50–51 above, 52–53 above, 56–57 above, 58–59 below, 60–61; Imperial War Museum London (Eileen Tweedy) 32–33 below; Peter Newark's Western Americana 25, 31; Octopus Library 54–55; The Tower of London Armouries 24 above; By Courtesy of the Victoria and Albert Museum, London (Sally Chappell) 16–17 above; The Museum of Artillery, Woolwich Contents, Introduction 6, 10–11, 12–13 below, 14–15, 20–21, 22 above, 23 above, 24 below, 26–27, 32–33 above, 34–35, 37–42 above, 43–49, 56–57 below, 58–59 above, 61 below, 62–63 below.

First published in 1980 by
Cathay Books
59 Grosvenor Street, London W1

ISBN 0 86178 059 0

Produced by Mandarin Publishers Ltd.
22a Westlands Road
Quarry Bay, Hong Kong

Printed in Hong Kong